RAKALI OF THE RIVERBANK

For my nature-loving sister Felice, and her grandkids Mikayla,
Jackson and Jasmine.
– SOR

For Indianna – in memory of her beloved rats Chilli and Lolly.
For River – for so many reasons.
– RG

NATIONAL LIBRARY OF AUSTRALIA

A catalogue record for this
book is available from the
National Library of Australia

ISBN: 9781486317547 (hbk)
ISBN: 9781486321544 (pbk)
ISBN: 9781486317554 (epdf)
ISBN: 9781486317561 (epub)

Published by:
CSIRO Publishing
36 Gardiner Road, Clayton VIC 3168
Private Bag 10, Clayton South VIC 3169
Australia

Telephone: +61 3 9545 8400
Email: publishing.sales@csiro.au
Website: www.publish.csiro.au
Sign up to our email alerts: publish.csiro.au/earlyalert

Edited by Dr Kath Kovac
Cover, text design and layout by Cath Pirret Design
Printed by Ingram Lightning Source

The views expressed in this publication are those of the author and illustrator and do not necessarily represent those of, and
should not be attributed to, the publisher or CSIRO.

CSIRO acknowledges the Traditional Owners of the lands that we live and work on across Australia and pays its respect to Elders
past and present. CSIRO recognises that Aboriginal and Torres Strait Islander peoples have made and will continue to make
extraordinary contributions to all aspects of Australian life including culture, economy and science. CSIRO is committed to
reconciliation and demonstrating respect for Indigenous knowledge and science. The use of Western science in this publication
should not be interpreted as diminishing the knowledge of plants, animals and environment from Indigenous ecological
knowledge systems.

Note for readers: Words in bold are explained in the glossary at the end of the book.

Note for teachers: Teacher notes are available at: https://www.publish.csiro.au/book/8115/#forteachers

RAKALI OF THE RIVERBANK

STEPHANIE OWEN REEDER ILLUSTRATED BY RACHEL GREGG

CSIRO PUBLISHING

Rakali's golden belly gleams
as rays of light kiss the river goodnight.
Danger lurks along the riverbank, but he's not afraid.

It's time to HUNT!

Rustling through the reeds, Rakali *GLIDES* into the water.
A cape of ripples flows out behind him.

He swims past a paddle of platypuses.
They're on the prowl too, searching for fat, juicy worms.

Flattening his ears, Rakali slips under the surface. He paddles with his webbed **hind feet**, steers with his strong tail and feels for **prey** with his sensitive whiskers.

DUCKING and DIVING, he chases
crustaceans lurking in the murky water.

GOTCHA!

The yabby's claws snap as Rakali
carries it back to his feeding rock.

He sits among the remains of earlier meals,
munching on the tasty treat.

Then his nose TWITCHES.

It's time to patrol his **territory**!
He spies his pups, who are playing beside the river.
Rakali does not stop.

He has **carcasses** to consume, foes to fight
and boundaries to **mark** with his smelly poo.

THWACK!

A humungous cane toad lands near the pups.
It's hungry, and eager for a snack.

The pups **SQUEAL** as their mother hisses a warning.

Heart hammering, Rakali rushes back.

He charges at the **toxic** toad,
sending the startled creature sprawling
on its back.

Quick as a flash, Rakali's teeth go snip, snip – SNAP!
Then he chomps on cane toad **innards**.

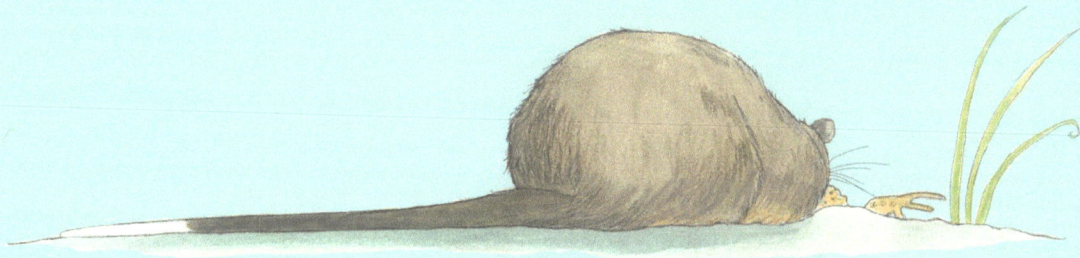

SNIFFLE! SNUFFLE!

Rakali roots through the leaf litter,
searching for **fungi** for dessert.

Moon shadows dance and a cool breeze ruffles his soggy fur.

Rakali SHIVERS.

It's time to head home to his burrow to warm up.

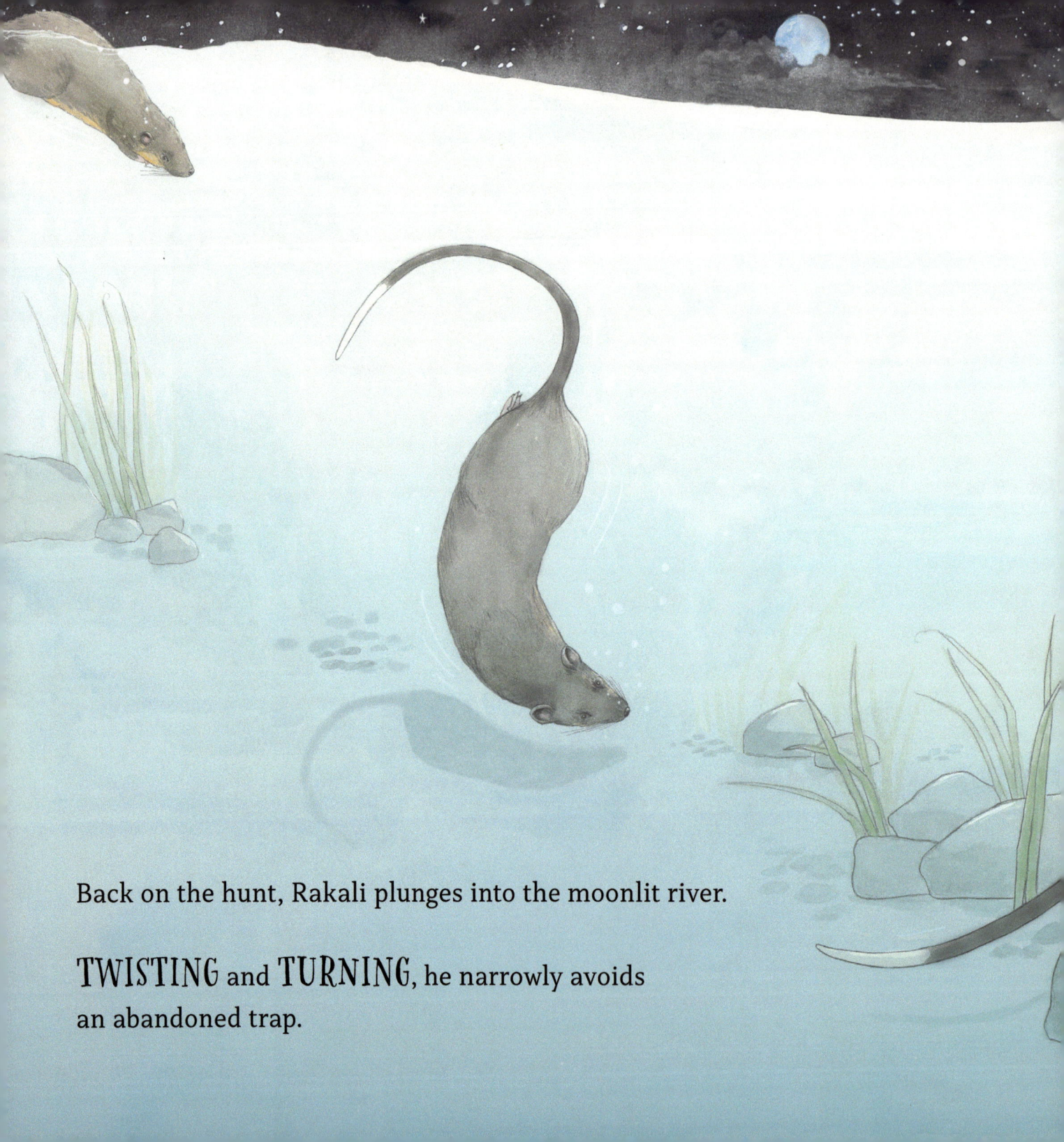

Back on the hunt, Rakali plunges into the moonlit river.

TWISTING and TURNING, he narrowly avoids
an abandoned trap.

But more dangers lurk nearby.

HISSSSS!

A huge carp tugs at Rakali's tail.

Will he be the winner?
Or will he end up as dinner?

After a fishy feast, Rakali cleans his whiskers
and scratches his bulging belly.

Then something RUSTLES in the bulrushes and his fur BRISTLES.

He finds footprints in a patch of gravelly sand.

CRUNCH!

The intruder squeals and skitters away – he won't be back!

Rakali SNIFFS the air.
Something else is skulking in the undergrowth –
a brooding presence, with silent paws and hungry eyes.

It's time to HIDE!

When it's safe, Rakali scurries back to his **midden**.
But more intruders have invaded his territory.
Hunkering down, he watches them, eyes aglow.

Then he POUNCES!

Dawn breaks and soft light bathes the river.
Rakali's job is done.

All's well on his patch of the riverbank.

It's time to SLEEP.

THE REMARKABLE RAKALI

WHAT IS A RAKALI?

The rakali is Australia's largest native **rodent**. Its scientific name is *Hydromys chrysogaster* (pronounced hy-dro-miss cry-so-gas-ter), and it is also known as a golden-bellied water mouse or native water rat. Indigenous people throughout Australia have different names for the water rat, including bud-bud (from the Ngarigu language), gurrumu (from the Yolngu language) and wampi (from the Ungaringyin language). The term rakali comes from the Ngarrindjeri people of the Murray River area of South Australia. In 1995, the Australian Nature Conservation Agency chose rakali as a more endearing name than water rat for these magnificent creatures.

The rakali is one of only two **amphibious mammals** in Australia. The other is the platypus (*Ornithorhynchus anatinus*). According to an Aboriginal Dreaming story, the platypus is the 'child' of a rakali and a black duck.

In personality and behaviour, rakali are more like otters than disease-carrying black rats (*Rattus rattus*). But European settlers treated rakali as pests and killed them. They also hunted them for their beautiful fur.

WHAT DO THEY LOOK LIKE?

Size: Around 60 centimetres long from nose to tip of tail — a bit larger than a platypus

Ears: Fold flat against their head when swimming

Eyes: Retroreflective, so they appear to glow in the dark when light shines on them

Body: Streamlined, and covered in **water-repellent** fur

Colour: Black, grey or brown fur on the back, with a white, tan, yellow or orange underbelly

Muzzle: Rounded, and bristling with super-sensitive whiskers

Teeth: Include a pair of sharp, chisel-shaped incisors at the front for cutting, and smooth molars at the back for grinding

Feet: Broad palms and sharp claws; hind feet are partly webbed

Tail: Long, muscular and dark-coloured, with a distinctive white tip

WHERE DO THEY LIVE?

Rakali are found in all Australian states and territories. They live beside **estuaries**, creeks, rivers, lakes and wetlands. Rakali have also been spotted in artificial waterways, such as Canberra's Lake Burley Griffin, and they sometimes hang out with the little penguins (*Eudyptula minor*) at St Kilda Pier in Melbourne.

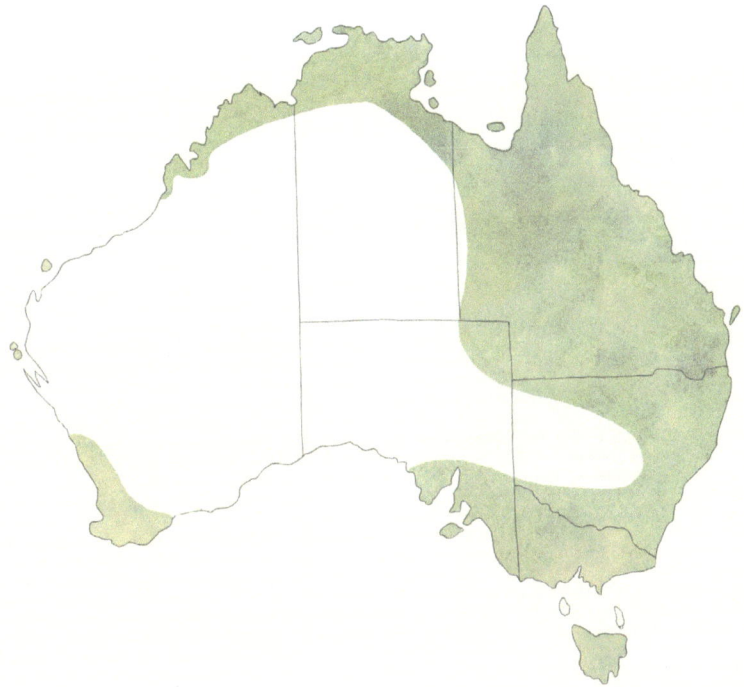

HOW DO THEY RAISE THEIR YOUNG?

Each spring, female rakali give birth to two to four pups. The pups are born in a grass-lined nest, inside a burrow beside a waterway. The mother raises the pups by herself while the male rakali patrols his territory, which can cover up to 4 kilometres. The male lives in a separate burrow to his mate – or mates – and her pups.

Rakali are usually solitary creatures. But when a group of them gets together, it's called a raft!

WHAT DO THEY EAT?

Rakali are mainly nocturnal, feeding at night from dusk to dawn. They hunt for fish, insects, crustaceans, shellfish, frogs, turtles, birds, water plants and fungi. After catching their prey, they take it back to a feeding platform on a rock or log, leaving behind a midden of shells, teeth, claws and bones. By eating animal carcasses, rakali help keep waterways clean. And the **fungal spores** in their poo help the rich river soil stay healthy.

Rakali also hunt **introduced species**, including black rats, carp and cane toads. They are one of only a few Australian native animals that have worked out how to safely kill these toxic toads. They avoid the poison glands on the toads' shoulders by knocking the creatures onto their backs. This allows them to get at the edible hearts and livers.

It's illegal to kill or relocate rakali, even when they annoy humans by pinching pets' dinners, stealing goldfish from garden ponds, killing backyard chickens, eating fish bait or leaving the gory remains of cane toads beside swimming pools.

WHAT THREATENS THEM?

Rakali are hunted by native **predators** such as snakes, large fish and birds of prey, as well as by **feral animals**, including foxes, cats and black rats. Other threats include human pollution of waterways, and loss of **habitat** from clearing land for farms and houses, or from droughts and floods. Rakali also get caught in fishing nets and traps. While the rakali is listed as Rare and Near Threatened in Western Australia, it is classified as Least Concern in the rest of the country.

. . . .

If you're lucky enough to spot a rakali in a waterway near you, report your sighting to the Australian Platypus Conservancy (https://platypus.asn.au). The information will be added to the Atlas of Living Australia database (https://www.ala.org.au). And you'll be helping scientists find out more about these remarkable Australian animals!

. . . .

GLOSSARY

. . . .

Amphibious mammals warm-blooded animals that give birth to their young and live both above and below the water

Carcasses the dead bodies of animals

Crustaceans hard-shelled animals that live in or near water, such as crabs, lobsters, prawns and yabbies

Estuaries the areas where large rivers run into the sea

Feral animals untamed animals not native to a country or a certain habitat

Fungal spores tiny, seed-like objects from which fungi grow

Fungi living things such as mushrooms, yeast and mould

Habitat the natural home or environment of an animal, plant or other living thing

Hind feet the back feet of a four-legged animal

Innards the inside organs of an animal, including the heart, lungs and liver

Introduced species animals not native to a country or a certain habitat

Mark to use pee, poo or other smelly substances to indicate the edges of an animal's territory

Midden a pile of leftover food including bones, teeth, claws and shells

Predators animals that hunt and kill other animals

Prey animals that are hunted and eaten by other animals

Rodent an animal with strong incisor teeth for gnawing food

Territory an area of land that an animal defends against intruders

Toxic harmful or poisonous

Water-repellent not easily penetrated by water, but not completely waterproof

ACKNOWLEDGEMENTS

Thank you to the editorial team at CSIRO Publishing and our scientific adviser Dr Marissa Parrott – Reproductive Biologist, Wildlife Conservation & Science at Zoos Victoria and Honorary Research Associate in BioScience at the University of Melbourne – for providing invaluable professional expertise during the creation of this book.

www.ingramcontent.com/pod-product-compliance
Lightning Source LLC
Chambersburg PA
CBHW042011080426
42734CB00002B/50